The Black Maze
The Steps Series

installations by Stan's Cafe

ISBN 978-1-913185-21-3

Published by Stan's Cafe
Birmingham, UK
2020

www.stanscafe.co.uk

The Black Maze © Stan's Cafe 2000
The Steps Series © Stan's Cafe 2008
The Black Maze photos
Opposite page 1 © Ed Dimsdale
Pages 3, 6, 8, 10, 11, 15 © James Yarker
Pages 12, 13 © Jake Oldershaw
Page 14 © Craig Stephens
Publication © Stan's Cafe 2020

Contents:

The Black Maze for promoters	1
The Black Maze story	2
Maze maps	16
The Steps Series	17

THE BLACK MAZE

www.stanscafe.co.uk

The Black Maze for rural touring promoters

What it is
The Black Maze is a unique audience adventure in the dark. Inspired by fairground rides and ancient mythology it is a labyrinth of dark twisting corridors, full of sound and lighting effects, mechanical tricks and physical puzzles. It has been described as 'a ghost train without the train', but nothing jumps out at you and the only monsters are the ones you take in yourself.

Its history
After proving a massive hit in art galleries, where it appealed equally to children, teenagers, adults and grandparents, the maze was re-built in the back of a 7.5 ton truck. Now it visits beaches, schools, festivals and market squares. It gets regular repeat bookings and occasionally travels abroad.

How it works
The Black Maze runs off batteries and comes with two helpful Maze Masters. Audiences enter alone or in pairs and navigate their way round the maze, mostly in the pitch black. They come out excited, shaken and delighted, desperate to share the experience with their friends. Children become obsessed, wanting to return time and again. Adults are surprised at the intensity of the experience and even sullen teenagers momentarily fail to be blasé when inside. An average of 25 people travel through the maze in an hour. It is the ideal focal point for a great social evening.

Yours for a day
The Black Maze is booked by the day. It can visit the local school in the afternoon and form the focus of a great social event in the evening. It can be parked in pub car parks, school playgrounds or outside village halls. It can be booked for village fetes or celebrations. People get personally involved in the maze, it is a challenge, creates a great buzz and many animated conversations. It is not as obvious as a theatre show, music concert or a dance and takes some imagination to book, but people will always remember the day the village was visited by *The Black Maze*.

The Black Maze **Story**

"I came across *The Black Maze* in Budapest when I went to the dentist there. It was brilliant and so unexpected, I wandered by chance to the truck in the street and watched people come out a little door in the back one by one, visibly affected by their experience. I had no idea what was inside, people were waiting to go in, it was very mysterious. Each person had to pass through the installation alone. It was like a mad dream inside, with the walls squeezing you and ethereal sounds being triggered by your movements, doors into different fractured dimensions, hidden doors, and clever manipulations of our normal senses. Altogether a top class show. Thanks."

Sarah Lovett

The Idea

The idea for *The Black Maze* had its origins, years before it was built, in Frontierland the Morecombe's windswept Wild West theme park. Normally when I tell this story I walk into a House Of Fun but a bit of research suggests maybe it was a Haunted Mine, which makes more sense as the entrance was a straight corridor, which got ever more gloomy the further you walked from daylight until, just beyond the point at which you couldn't see where you were going, the corridor took a turn to the right, jolting your left shoulder and correcting your path. This jolt to the shoulder triggered a shock of adrenaline no less powerful than that prompted by the nearby rollercoaster but with a far greater economy of means.

The simplicity of the dark corridor's power caused me to speculate; if that were just the start of a sensory adventure in the dark what would the rest of it be like? How much adrenaline would you need to pass through a black maze?

This idea hung suspended for years until promoter Alan James enquired about booking our hit show *It's Your Film* for an event he was planning as part of Birmingham's Millennium Celebrations. The event, called *Revolution*, was to take place on the 2nd and 3rd of January 2000 and Alan agreed that commissioning a new piece was much more apt for this event than booking an old one, so *The Black Maze* was go!

The Dimensions

Our initial plan was to build *The Black Maze* in a 20' x 8' shipping container, so it could be plug-and-go at the International Convention Centre without any get-in time and from there we could take it anywhere to anyone who may want it. It was only after we had come up with a design and started construction in a shipping container that enquiries started to suggest that getting a shipping container delivered anywhere on 2nd January, 2000 was going to be impossible for any sane price. A rethink was required. We stripped out what we had already installed in the container, booked some workshop space and started building *The Black Maze* again, this time as if it were a theatre set folded in on itself.

The Design

The Black Maze's name is doubly misleading as it is neither a maze nor black.

We'd never intended to give anyone a choice of directions in *The Black Maze as* we couldn't afford to have people lost for hours inside and untaken paths would squander precious space. We needed to create a single path that would be challenging to find in places but always ensure that visitors pass through every one of the installation's 160 square feet.

By experimenting we discovered that distances walked in the pitch black feel longer than they do when you can see where you're going. This was good news for us. What would be better still is if we could get visitors to pass along the same corridor twice, in different directions, without knowing they had done so, we could then make the entrance door double as the exit door and in so doing both save space and add a 'magical' feel to the experience.

Our big breakthrough came when we recognised that a door opened 90° blocks off the space behind it. We could thus use an open door to block off a corridor we didn't want visitors to walk down. In this way we could route people across a corridor they've already walked down and send them back out along the entrance corridor. By adding sound and lighting effects to the exit journey this single corridor could be given two different characters.

Whilst *The Black Maze* would be predominantly black, to deny ourselves visuals effects entirely seemed unduly restricting. We decided to allow occasional, carefully placed visual effects after an initial long pitch black section.

The Aspiration
From the start we were clear that we weren't building a Haunted House; our objective wasn't to scare visitors. We appreciated that *The Black Maze* may be scary but we liked the idea that any monsters found in the maze should only be those taken in by the visitors themselves. People should only be scared by themselves; their own thoughts, the unexpected sight of themselves or the echoing sound of themselves.

In preparing promotional material I found myself getting drawn into marketing hyperbole and writing about 'facing down and overcoming fears' and 'undergoing a rite of passage'. These were nice thoughts, but perhaps too much to live up to?

The Technology
We recruited artist Mark Anderson to devise and build the maze with us and he in turn recruited Graeme Calvert, his partner in performance company Blissbody, to solve some of our more baffling electrical challenges. Alone we could build a wobbly floor and drill thousands of tiny holes through plywood to create stars when lights shine behind them and mount mirrors so they reflect in an infinite regression in five directions; we could combine fans with fabric to make walls that swell out and have to be pushed through; we could turf a small room with real turf and mount infra-red lights, an infra-red camera and a Pepper's Ghost to float someone's face in front of them in space in the dark and we could tape contact microphones to the reverse sides of wall panels to make any scuff, scrape or bang made by fingers, elbows or hips echo back on the scuffer, scraper or banger; but to make all the lights and samples switch on and off when this pressure pad was trodden on or that door was opened or closed was a job for Graeme and the circuitry he put in those mysterious pale blue boxes.

The Build
Our workshop was cold but my memory is that the building process went fairly smoothly. Our carpentry skills were rudimentary but inside everything would be painted black and outside everything would be draped in black cloth, so the finish didn't have to look slick, it just had to fit together and feel smooth to the touch at hand level. In the run up to New Year's day we labelled every piece of our maze, took it apart and stowed it in a hired Luton van.

The ICC
We arrived at the International Convention Centre early on 2nd January and drove our van directly into Hall 3 where we were to re-build the maze. We bolted all the wooden panels together and placed all the electronic components in their designated locations, then ran bell wire to connect everything up. A feature of the electronic system was that when first the power was

switched on every sample would begin playing and someone would have to take a journey through the maze for everything to set itself. By now we were so familiar with the layout there was no need to put the working/emergency lights on. A second trip through confirmed everything was working, so we draped the whole structure in black fabric, hung up our The Black Maze sign, and announced that we were ready to open for business.

The Audience
Audiences instantly loved *The Black Maze*, people went in nervous and came out exhilarated. Some said they had faced down and overcome their fear of the dark or confined spaces or both, someone even said it felt like a rite of passage; my promotional copy was not too hyperbolic after all.

Most people spoke about their time in *The Black Maze* as a challenge but we were always very gratified by those who said they found their journey comforting and enjoyable. Our intention had always been for the journey to be exciting and exploratory, rather than a race to get through and out. Audiences appreciated this and would often ask to undertake a second trip in order to spend more time playing and less time being anxious about getting lost.

The Invigilation
We developed a briefing for visitors the script for which went something like this, "Welcome to The Black Maze. You shouldn't be able to get lost as there is always a way through. Never turn back. When you see a corridor full of stars follow that and it will bring you home. If you want to get out early just shout and we'll come and get you".

We had microphones positioned throughout the maze connected to an ear piece so we could hear how people were getting on, but listening to the sequenced banging of doors and playing of samples we generally knew where people were without this aid. On the rare occasions people did call to be rescued we would usually resist switching on the emergency lights and ruining the atmosphere, instead we'd dive in with a torch, using our knowledge of the doors and their tricks to take short cuts to the scene of the problem.

For audiences queuing outside to go in, the banging and samples, along with occasional squeals and shrieks, served to heighten their anticipation of what was to come.

An average journey time through the maze was about four minutes. Initially we attempted to be firm in our insistence that

The Black Maze was to be experienced alone, one person at a time. Later we realised that this rule was putting off people who would otherwise enjoy the experience. We were persuaded that two people going through together had a different but still valid experience. It was bonding for them and boosted our audience numbers, so we grew more relaxed about allowing two friends in at a time, so long as they keep close together.

The Black Maze rarely caused panic. Once inside visitors knew almost instantly if the experience would be too dark or claustrophobic for them and step straight back out. The rare exceptions came when a confident friend, having pressurised a scared friend to go in with them, then lost confidence and grew scared themselves. This would trigger a strong reaction from the originally scared friend and on these occasions we had to be quick with the torch and the reassuring words. Scared visitors never held a grudge against the maze, they saw the fear as their own failing.

Looking after *The Black Maze* was fun. It was technically and physically robust and so rarely caused problems. Talking to people before they went in and absorbing their reactions when they came out was always enjoyable.

The Tour
After its initial outing the maze was packed flat and put into storage in the expectation that it may have a future life. Within weeks Craftspace had booked it for almost a month as part of *Coming To Our Senses*, an exhibition at Birmingham's Gas Hall. From there it went directly to Nottingham for four days at the Freefall and Now festivals. The following year *The Black Maze* was at the Site Gallery in Sheffield for a fortnight and then at the De la Warr pavilion in Bexhill-on-Sea for a long weekend.

The Conversion

Whilst invigilating *The Black Maze* in Sheffield, I met a group of young people who had been brought to the gallery as part of a drugs rehabilitation programme. They explained that they'd not been to a gallery before and quizzed me about our black draped monolith, "Is it art?" I said I thought it was, but that it wouldn't bother me if they didn't think it was, so long as they liked it, whatever it was. Well they did like it, very much, and that weekend a number of them returned with their friends and families to join the queue alongside delegates of a Live Art conference being held at the Gallery.

Even before this encounter we'd talked about rebuilding *The Black Maze* in the back of a lorry. Despite getting better at putting the maze together installation still took a day and the get out hours, which meant any booking had to be substantial enough to warrant the effort, plus all this fitting up, taking down, transport and storage was causing wear and damage. Now we had an example of a group of people who would never normally visit a gallery, but who loved *The Black Maze*. If the maze were in the back of a lorry it could visit to them.

The Lorry

As *The Black Maze* was originally designed to fit inside a 20' x 8' shipping container its dimensions were close to those of the box on the back of a standard 7.5 ton truck and this was largest vehicle any of the more senior members of Stan's Cafe could legally drive without the need for more training and tests. We suggested to Arts Council England that they should cover the cost of buying a second hand truck and we should cover the conversion costs, they agreed, we found an old Royal Mail lorry and work began.

The conversion was more complicated than it sounds. The existing maze was constructed from the outside and this one had to be built from the inside. The back end of the lorry caused us the most work. The roller shutter was replaced by swing doors, we built wooden steps and a roof to bridge between these doors when they were open and added railings. Finally the lorry was resprayed from Royal Mail red to white and *The Black Maze* logo added.

On The Road

And so The Black Maze started its second life. It could park up on any level street, village green or town square, drop its tail lift, hook up to some 13amp power and welcome visitors. Initially it roamed across England but eventually was invited to Scotland, Ireland, Northern Ireland, Greece, France and Hungary.

It did corporate gigs indoors in Brighton and it was invited to the National Theatre in London.

Audience As Performers

In the final scene of our 270 second long performance *It's Your Film* (1998) its two actors have disappeared into the darkness, leaving just the single audience member watching their own reflection, framed in front of a projection that makes them appear to be in the back seat of a car, being driven through a city at night in the rain.

What I find attractive in this moment is that the audience member is acting for themselves as the narrative's missing third figure; they are simultaneously both actor and audience. *The Black Maze* seeks to pull a similar trick but without any other actors at all.

The Black Maze corridor twists from being theatrical set into theatrical narrative. The duration of the performance is simply the time it takes each audience member to pass through the set. As an actor's performance improves when they grow more familiar with their script, so audience's improve their performances as they revisit *The Black Maze*. A common theme was for visitors to say their first journey through the maze was a survival course or physical puzzle, they simply tried to get through as fast as they could. Of their second visit they claimed to be more relaxed, more confident and sure of themselves, as a consequence they were able to explore the maze and its resonances more thoroughly. Despite my intimate knowledge of the maze I continued to enjoy journeying through it, acting my way round, pretending to be surprised, intrigued and delighted. Just as one enjoys re-watching favourite films, re-listening to music one likes or re-reading a much loved book, so passing through The Black Maze remained fun to the end.

Maintenance and the end of The Black Maze

Long term parking for *The Black Maze* was tricky to arrange. We made an agreement with the Parcel Force depot across the road from our rehearsal space. When that closed Cadbury

World let us use the far end of their car park in exchange for a couple of days open for their visitors. Finally our new landlords A E Harris & Co. Ltd. let us use their car park.

Each year we had to pay road tax, MOT, servicing and insurance on *The Black* Maze, it was the only element of our portfolio that cost us money even when we weren't performing it! People still loved it but we didn't have the administrative capacity we needed to get the bookings we needed to make the money we needed to justify keeping it on the road.

After eight years in the lorry and ten years in total we finally scrapped *The Black Maze*.

Maze Maps

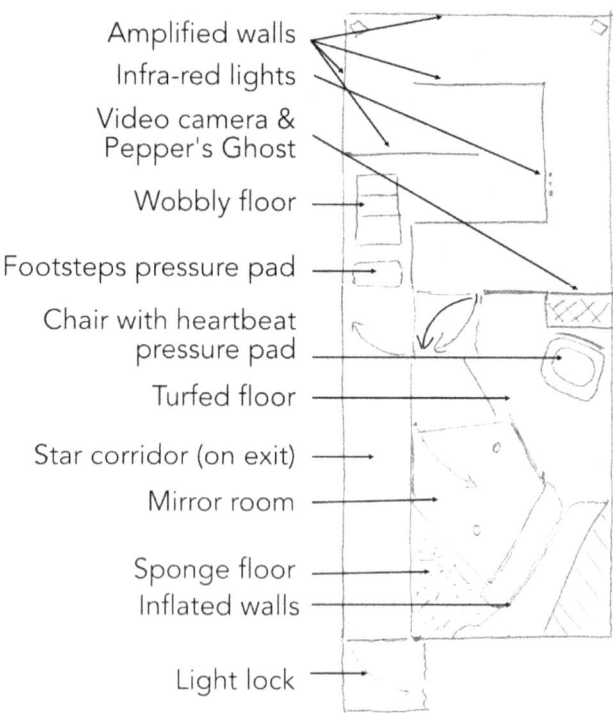

- Amplified walls
- Infra-red lights
- Video camera & Pepper's Ghost
- Wobbly floor
- Footsteps pressure pad
- Chair with heartbeat pressure pad
- Turfed floor
- Star corridor (on exit)
- Mirror room
- Sponge floor
- Inflated walls
- Light lock

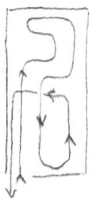

When visitors followed the advice they were given before entry, "never turn back, there's always a way through," then this is the route they should find. Note the cross over and the stretch of corridor used in two directions.

The Steps Series

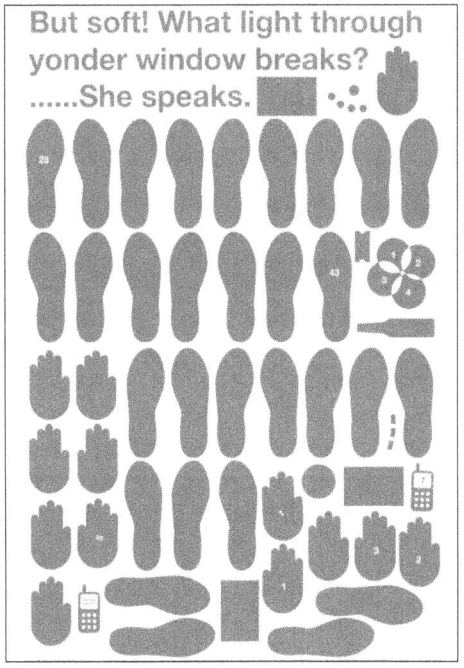

Dance Steps
MAC, Birmingham 31st March - 6th April, 2008

Our idea for a teach-yourself-theatre vinyl installation was long standing, we'd just been waiting for an opportunity to make it, so when MAC asked us to make a piece to mark its closure for rebuilding we knew what to suggest. The story of a woman's life, told through her engagement with the arts centre, featuring scenes spread throughout the building, was a means to remind people of all the activities undertaken in the venue and its significance in their lives.

As our first attempt at creating vinyl instructions for audiences to act out a drama for themselves, *Dance Steps* was where we developed our new grammar, it was also when we learnt the techniques and skills of adhesive vinyl application.

Scene 1: Staircase to Randle Studio. A couple are kissing.
Scene 2: The Cafe (upper level). A relationship ends.
Scene 3: Women's Toilets (upstairs). Two friends chat. "You're

better off without him"

Scene 4: Balcony above The Hexagon. A child asks "Why does that man look sad?"

Scene 5: Box Office (right hand side). Tickets for the cinema.

Scene 6: The Bar. There is a spark "He's coming over!"

Scene 7: Arts Balcony. Flirting, a couple play at Shakespeare.

Scene 8: Painting and Drawing Studio. Still life with dance.

Scene 9: Women's Toilets (downstairs). A pregnant woman is sick, "Are you alright in there?"

Scene 10: The Cafe (lower level). Parental tension with pushchair and child.

Scene 11: Inner Courtyard (pay phone). A teenager calls home, "He's watching me!"

Scene 12: Box Office (left hand side). Tickets for the theatre.

Scene 13: The Hexagon Theatre. An elderly couple watch *Romeo and Juliet*, the lovers die.

Scene 14: Outside the Cinema. Two old friends reflect on a visit to the cinema years ago.

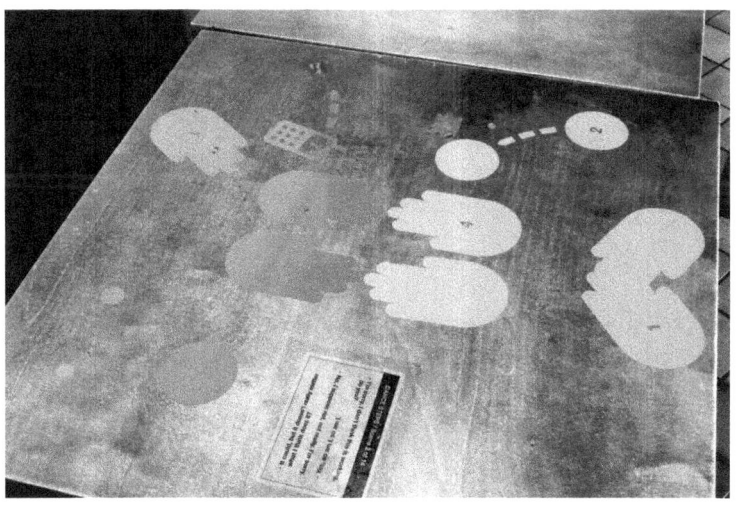

Devised by Simon Ford, Craig Stephens and James Yarker.
Installed with help from Kaylie Black and Karen Stafford.
Photographs © Ed Dimsdale.

Spy Steps
Warwick Arts Centre, Coventry 28th May - 26th June, 2009

The success of *Dance Steps* led to a commission from Warwick Arts Centre and encouraged us to buy a plotter, so we could cut our own vinyl. Cutting our own vinyl on-site made the project cheaper and more flexible, allowing us to be more ambitious.

The architecture of MAC had required an episodic approach but the large open spaces of WAC allowed for unbroken action with audience members able to choose which of four main roles they wished to play (blue, green, red or yellow footprints). The university campus inspired us to recast the WAC as headquarters to an evil genius bent on world domination; the perfect setting for the final scenes of a James Bond style film.

We had an Aston Matin crashing through the venue's plate glass doors, machine gun fire, our hero knocked unconscious and rescued, a roulette table, a frantic climb, a hand going for the gun only to have the gun kicked away and finally, the missile silo destroyed by limpet mines as our hero and his saviour leave the building through its other glass doors.

With a through-line of action it became possible to have a soundtrack. With headphones and an MP3 player visitors could follow the blue path with breaking glass, machine gun fire, cosh, roulette wheel and limpet mine sound effects all synching with your performance of *Spy Steps*.

Devised by Simon Ford, Craig Stephens and James Yarker, with help from Denise Stanton. Soundtrack by Nina West. Photographs © Andrew Billington.

49 Steps
Dance Base, Edinburgh 25th - 29th August, 2009

It is Scotland, an international conference (possibly a peace conference), is taking place just beneath Edinburgh's famous castle. Media interest is high. Delegates are quizzed on their way in. Security is tight. A woman with an urgent message is repelled, but jumps the service lift and disguises herself as a member of the catering team.

Meanwhile, a man sneaks in through a fire exit. He sets his briefcase down at a table and quizzes two old diplomats sat chatting. "Gluten free canapés for the Manx delegation?" the fake waitress asks, "there is no Manx delegation".

Our two main protagonists collide in the corridor, briefcase and canapés fly. She overhears delegates talking, they mention the Manx delegate, she recalls talk of forty nine steps and runs to the roof.

Someone has sprayed paint over the security camera and assembled a sniper's rifle from his briefcase.

She has run to the top floor, but by this route it's only twenty one steps. Across the roof she sees the assassin poised but a locked door bars her way. The professor is making her way to the platform to speak. "Wait!" Rachel Hannay is held and as she tells her story word comes of an unconscious waitress in a lift. Rachel sheds her jacket and flees through the conference room. She pounds up the stairs, the professor decides to take the stage, looking down from the forty ninth step through the conference hall's glass roof the sniper nearly has the professor in his sights. Rachel arrives, there is a tussle, the rifle flies, when security finally plods into view she has everything under control.

In an attempt to win more bookings for what we now envisaged as *The Steps Series*, we installed an edition at Dance Base, the hub of the British Council Showcase, at the Grass Market in Edinburgh. The building's glass roof with its view of the castle, the Scottish location and international delegation prompted us to use John Buchan's adventure novel, *The 39 Steps*, as our inspiration. We adapted his title before discovering, to our shock, that there are precisely 49 steps from the venue's entrance to its top most level from which, looking down into the main dance studio through a window, our assassination attempt would take place. This edition tested how we could build an installation using the architecture of an unusual building, while also avoiding disrupting the function of that building. We were pleased with what felt like a very elegant solution.

Devised by Simon Ford, Craig Stephens and James Yarker.
Photographs © Jannica Honey.

Giant Steps
@ A E Harris, Birmingham, September 2009

In the first three editions we had noticed how much young children loved playing with the steps, even though the content wasn't aimed at them, the stride lengths were too long and the footprints too big. It felt like time to make an edition especially for this younger audience.

At that time Stan's Cafe had a big factory space as its venue, so we decided to make *Giant Steps* there. The heart of the show was the Jack and the Beanstalk story marked out in vinyl. Additional fairytale elements were added around this central story: a girl being turned into a frog by a witch and jumping around on lily pads before being turned back into a girl and then a princess, by a prince riding in on a horse; Jack's cow traded for beans then runs away to jump over the moon, with attendant crowd of laughing dog, dish, spoon, cat and fiddle; there was also a rope skipping game, a Miss Muffet, a pirate guarding treasure, a maypole and a maze.

With the age of our audience in mind we almost entirely dispensed with dialogue and made sure the piece had lots of open choices and free flowing action in its footpaths.

Devised by Simon Ford and James Yarker,
with help from Denise Stanton, Abi Duffty and Jack Trow.
Soundtrack by Nina West.
Photographs © Jonathan Stokes

Odyssey Steps
Croydon Clocktower, September - October 2009

Croydon Clocktower is a venue combining a library, museum, performance hall/cinema and cafe. Part of our commissioning brief was to promote the opening of a new public entrance to the hall. The fact that this entrance, directly off the street, prevented audiences having to make an epic journey through the venue to find the hall was all the inspiration we required.

Odysseus has returned from the Trojan wars with his warriors and is due to meet Penelope for a trip to the theatre. After building himself a raft and navigating through various trials involving a cyclops, sirens, lotus eaters, the isle of Calypso and a trip to the Western Edge of the World, he finally arrives outside the theatre, only to discover Penelope is already there ready to give him a hard time. She had nipped in via the new entrance ages ago and has just sent their son off to find his dad.

Our epic source material encouraged spectacular visuals meaning the installation could work as a piece of visual art, to be appreciated even by those not actively engaging with it as instructions for a performance.

The big technical innovation within *Odyssey Steps* was Simon Ford developing a speech bubble design that made dialogue much easier to integrate into our do-it-yourself performance.

Devised by Simon Ford and James Yarker
With Denise Stanton and Jack Trow
Photographs © Stan's Cafe

Space Steps
Beaumont Leys School, Leicester. From November, 2009

When we first saw the brand new building housing Beaumont Leys School we knew it would make a superb canvas for an edition of *The Steps* Series. A team of students and teachers visited *Spy Steps* with us to get ideas. Students pitched ideas for the project's theme. The challenge of changing this futuristic looking school into a spaceship was irresistible.

Our student team helped guide the structure and narrative of *Space Steps*. The adventure starts at the building's front entrance, where robot guards slide aside to allow admission. From here the piece follows a smooth route around the building concluding on the top floor with the flight deck. Banks of lockers became incubation units for aliens and storage facilities for the elements. Music rooms became fuel tanks. Stowaways attempt to steal the Diamond Drive, aliens escape and have to be recaptured, General Teaching arrives and the crew prepare to make a jump to hyperspace.

Our student team came in over half term to install the piece in secret and provide a surprise for students returning from their holidays. Having helped us design and install *Space Steps*, our student team maintained it and provided guided tours for parents, visitors and their peers. Many teachers used the piece as stimulus for their teaching

Devised by Simon Ford, Craig Stephens and James Yarker,
with Denise Stanton and Rheanna Boyes, Kieran Figg,
Vinay Jamnadas, Jasmin Kaur, Jemini Pandya, Ashika Pattni,
Ranko Radulovic and Georgia Whitaker,
with Ms. Livesley, Ms Hicken and Ms Hall.
Alien / Robot Designs by classes 9RLH and 7SB.

Sound Design by Lovedeep Bharaj, Coutney Bliss,
Rosie-Olivier Heggs, Bhavik Solanki, Annabelle Tarrant and
Ross Westbrook with Angus Wallace.

Produced by Miss. Crosby and Andrew Fox.
Commissioned by The Mighty Creative.

Photographs © Andrew Billington.

Final Steps
@ A E Harris, Birmingham, January - May, 2010

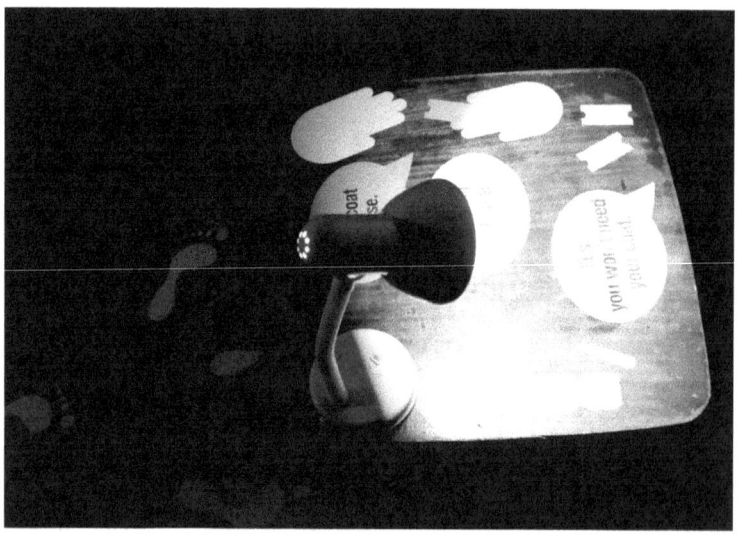

As *The Steps Series* was inspired by teach-yourself-to-dance floor mats, we leapt at the chance to make a version for the British Dance Edition showcase. One of the features of the installation is that it can be read from the outside, as notation for movement and voices, but at its best it only makes complete sense when audiences place their hands and feet on the vinyl prints and embody the piece. The same is true of play scripts versus productions but surely applies more strongly to notation and dance.

We were hosting dance companies in the larger spaces of our home venue so for *Final Steps* we challenged ourselves to make a miniature, a 'chamber piece'. By way of compensation we were able to select and arrange furniture and props and utilise a staircase leading to a cellar.

Barefoot you gain consciousness outside a nightclub. Security is expecting you. Inside an old friend begs for money and a limping man asks for a light. "I don't smoke" you reply, "Not yet" they say. A dwarf standing on a ladder smartens you up. A band plays a lopsided tango, its singer is an old flame of yours and the barman knows your order already. A ring is returned to you and wagered on the turn of a card - it's a skull. A giant bars your exit and the cloakroom attendant takes your coat as you leave "you won't need it".

Through a side door a vicious dog on a chain forces you to turn left. A staircase descends into smoke and infernal noise, you evaporate on the top step.

Devised by Simon Ford, Amanda Hadingue, Craig Stephens and James Yarker
Sound Design by Nina West
Photographs © Alicja Rogalska

Market Steps
Southside Shopping Centre, Wandsworth
29th April - 23rd May, 2010

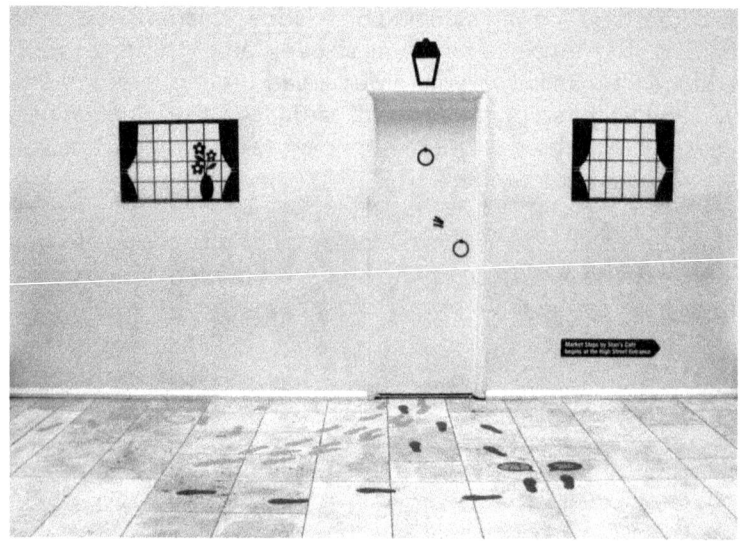

Less than a year after *Odyssey Steps* we were invited to make a new edition of *The Steps Series* barely a mile down the road, at Southside Shopping Centre, Wandsworth

On a site visit our thoughts turned to how the phrase shopping centre could once have referred to a market square in a small town. We thought it would be fun to try and reimagine this modern space in that historic way. The success of *Giant* Steps made us keen to place child protagonists at the heart of *Market Steps*. We had recently read Catherine O'Flynn's novel *What Was Lost* which centres on a child detective and a shopping centre. The idea of a child detective in a public space in turn made us think of Erich Kastner's novella *Emile and the Detectives* and we drew inspiration from there.

"There are animals wandering the Southside Shopping Centre, chewing on grass, treading on flowers and generally doing what animals do. It's market day and from miles around people have brought their produce for sale. It should be a peaceful scene, but there is a thief on the loose and the local children are out to catch him."

In order not disrupt life and commerce in the centre we avoided vinyl needing to go on any shop windows and prepared ourselves so thoroughly that we were able to install the entire piece overnight, when the centre was closed to the public.

> # stan'scafe
>
> ## I SPY: MARKET STEPS
>
> At the High Street entrance of Southside, a series of vinyl footprints mark the start of Market Steps. With your feet on those footprints and using your imagination you should be able to start acting out the story of Market Steps. You will have to search for each element of the story as you walk through the shopping centre. In addition to working out the story you may want to tick off these things as you find them.
>
> | | |
> |---|---|
> | ☐ A snail | ☐ A telescope |
> | ☐ A bird flying | ☐ An owl |
> | ☐ A flower | ☐ A bone |
> | ☐ A skipping rope | ☐ Someone being lifted off the ground |
> | ☐ A book | ☐ Someone changing shoes |
> | ☐ Hoof prints from a horse | ☐ A collision |
> | ☐ A pig eating | ☐ A fight |
> | ☐ A butterfly | ☐ A musical instrument |
> | ☐ A bird's nest | ☐ A cockerel |
>
> Made by Simon Ford and James Yarker
> With Chris Dugrenier and Denise Stanton
> Design by Simon Ford
> With thanks to Neil Churchill, Alex Herbert, Helen Renwick and Graeme Rose
>
> Stan's Cafe is a theatre company, based in Birmingham, which specialises in making unusual theatre shows.
>
> www.stanscafe.co.uk   southside   ARTS COUNCIL ENGLAND

Devised by Simon Ford and James Yarker,
with Denise Stanton and Chris Dugrenier.
Commissioned by the Wandsworth Arts Festival.
With thanks to: Neil Churchill, Alex Herbert,
Helen Renwick, Graeme Rose
Photograph © Stan's Cafe

Revolutionary Steps
The National Theatre, London 5th - 31st August, 2010

The Black Maze had appeared at The National Theatre in 2008, parked up outside as part of the venue's *Watch This Space* programme of free public attractions. Two years later we were invited inside. Büchner's play *Danton's Death* was being staged in the Olivier Theatre and our challenge was to adapt it into vinyl instructions, so audiences could perform it in the theatre's foyer spaces.

The challenge this act of compression represented was compounded by the fact that carpets and textured concrete walls made large areas of the venue's public spaces unsuited to applying vinyl; we had to be inventive and resourceful.

REVOLUTIONARY ■ ▌ STEPS

This programme will help you discover the Revolutionary Steps scenes scattered through the Olivier side of the building. The vinyl colours of central characters in particular scenes are highlighted below, supporting characters are represented by various other colours.

We hope you enjoy solving the vinyl puzzles and performing your own version of Revolutionary Steps.

SCENE 1: (Ground Floor Foyer, Concert Pitch)
Prologue. King Louis XVI (Yellow) is executed and Danton (Red) and Robespierrre (Blue) are feted by the crowds.

SCENE 2: (Outside Mezzanine Restaurant)
Despite the revolution there remains a gap between rich and poor.

SCENE 3: (Balcony, Olivier Cloakroom Level 1)
Danton (Red) and Robespierre (Blue) discuss the progress of the revolution.

SCENE 4: (Toilet Lobby, Olivier Cloakroom Level 1)
Members of the Committee of Public Safety (Green) and Robespierre (Blue) plot to arrest Danton.

SCENE 5: (Olivier Cloakroom, Level 1)
Danton (Red) is arrested.

SCENE 6: (Terrace Doors, Level 1)
Danton (Red) appears before the Revolutionary Tribunal.

SCENE 7: (Lift, Terrace Entrance Level 1)
A plot to rig the jury at Danton's trial.

SCENE 8: (Window, Level 2, Olivier Stalls Bar Right)
Danton's wife Julie (Red) laments the arrest of her husband.

SCENE 9: (Window, Level 2, Olivier Stalls Bar Left)
Danton (Red) and Camille (Purple) share their last moments together in prison.

SCENE 10: (Centre Windows, Olivier Stalls Level 2)
Danton (Red) and Camille (Purple) are executed.

SCENE 11: (Window, Olivier Circle Bar Level 3)
Julie decides she does not want to live without Danton.

SCENE 12: (Centre Windows, Olivier Circle Level 3)
Camille's wife Lucile faces a life without her husband.

SCENE 13: (Centre Windows, Olivier Circle Level 3)
Lucile is arrested.

Devised by: Simon Ford, Craig Stephens and James Yarker
Installed by: Simon Ford, Denise Stanton and Craig Stephens
Thanks to Angus and Emily at Watch This Space and to all the staff of The National Theatre for accommodating this temporary addition to their building.

Photograph © Stan's Cafe

Apollo Steps
Domaine d'O, Montpelier, France
2nd - 30th October, 2010

The dry weather of Montpellier and polished concrete of Domaine d'O's amphitheatre encouraged this first outdoor edition of *The Steps Series*.

The venue's seasons were being programmed by phases of the moon, the Greek style amphitheatre's curved stage reminded us of a lunar surface and its high black back wall suggested a night sky; everything pointed towards *Apollo Steps*
.
Here three stories of aspiration run in parallel:

A young child looks at the moon through a telescope and vows to walk on its surface. We follow them through university, physical training, rocket launch and setting foot on the moon. Unseen by many a mouse has done the same journey looking for cheese.

A child visits a big concert and vows to perform on that stage. We find her at school, playing and singing. We witness her band splitting up and her skim a demo disc to a manager through a crowd at stage door. Finally we and catch up with her in the wings as she goes on for her first big concert. Her mother is in the front row.

A shy violinist meets a prima ballerina back stage and she says that one day he will be a soloist too. They marry. She grows frail and they attend a concert together. She dies. He attends her funeral before retaking his place as first violinist in the orchestra. As he plays he sees his wife dancing once again.

Devised by Simon Ford and James Yarker,
with Denise Stanton and Chris Dugrenier.
Translation Charlotte Gregory. Soundscape by Nina West.
Photographs © Stan's Cafe.

Sandwell Steps
The Public - West Bromwich 6th July - 18th September, 2011

Sandwell Steps was commissioned as part of the gallery's Alan Ahlberg exhibition. It responded to the building's unusual architecture, Allan Ahlberg's children's stories and an interview with the author. Throughout, children play make-believe games in parallel with the adult world and are regularly told to 'stop being silly', eventually they meet a storyteller who encourages them to tell 'wonderfully silly stories'.

Scene 1: In the Town Square an adult and infant play Peepo and older children play monsters.

Scene 2: Children tease a park keeper by pretending to be dogs. An adult couple kiss.

Scene 3: A snow angel, toboggan ride, snowball fight, an elderly person slips, a carrot is stolen for a Snowman.

Scene 4: In Mrs. Lather's Laundry all manner of creatures are being washed.

Scene 5: At the Railway Station a child is evacuated to Worcester and a family arrive from India.

Scene 6: Grandad digs up carrots in the allotment, a child pretends to be a rabbit, another digs up treasure.

Scene 7: In the Graveyard, looking at the stars a child imagines two skeletons exchanging spare parts.

Scene 8: Flowers are placed beside the canal and a ghost child climbs out of the far side.

Scene 9: The Bus Stop: a child refuses to move up because their dead brother is sitting between them.

Scene 10: Outside the factory adults queue for work while children play football, imagining it's a cup final.

Scene 11: Two teachers watch on as children play a range of playground games.

Scene 12: At the launch of a ship two pirates have a huge cutlass fight, until their mum tells them to behave.

Scene 13: Surrounded by a class of aliens a daydreaming child spots a Flying Saucer out of the window. Their teacher is unimpressed.

Scene 14: A burglar climbs into a bedroom and steals a painting but perhaps this is just a dream.

Scene 15: After the storyteller finishes, it's the children's turn to make something up.

Devised by Simon Ford, Craig Stephens and James Yarker, with help from Kerrie Reading, Denise Stanton and Harry Trow.
Commissioned by Ian Danby and Graham Peet.
Photograph © Stan's Cafe

Olympian Steps.
Handsworth and Aston Parks
24th March - 24th September,ß 2012

The London 2012 Olympics and our discovery of biodegradable paint allowed the first documentary edition of *The Steps Series* to be installed in Aston and Handsworth parks, in North Birmingham.

Our objective was to allow visitors to follow in the gold medal winning footsteps of famous Olympians and gain a more realistic sense of their achievements. We studied videos and the record books carefully and carried a long tape measure to the parks in order mark out on the paths there, on a 1:1 scale, just how far Tessa Sanderson's javelin flew, how Bob Beamon jumped, how long Usain Bolt's stride length was and how Olga Korbut's hands and feet fuelled those tumbles.

It was an elegant and satisfying piece that met with much public interest. The installation, using stencils, was laborious but not unduly difficult.

Devised by Simon Ford, Craig Stephens and James Yarker,
with help from Jack Trow.
Thanks to: Lee Southall - Birmingham Parks Department,
Friends of Aston Park, Staff of Aston Hall,
Jesse Gerald, Ana Rutter, Pat Whyte
Supported by Birmingham City Council.
Photographs © Stan's Cafe

Mystery Steps
Coventry Mysteries, Coventry City Centre
9th - 16th June, 2012

Coventry Mysteries Week commissioned an edition of *The Steps Series* and found us a vacant cafe unit to work in. It made sense to use the unit's existing features for the installation and so, to also chime with the week's mediaeval heritage, we created a comic vision of what a cafe in that era could have been.

Out back a chef is asleep in the stores and someone's butchering a pig. Children are hard at work with the washing up, waiting and turning the spit. Out front a host of customers are having fun, queuing for the latest delicacies and playing local sports, meanwhile a team are enacting a mystery play in the cafe's window, for gathered passers-by. Their show is about a miracle, loaves and fishes from a boy's packed lunch are used to feed five thousand people.

Devised by Simon Ford, Denise Stanton and James Yarker,
with Craig Stephens and Christina M Kruise.
Installed by Simon Ford, Denise Stanton,
Alice Greenham and Chris Dugrenier.
With thanks to: Hannah Grainger and Johnny O'Hanlon.
Supported by Coventry City Council.
Photographs © Stan's Cafe.

Golden Steps, London
22nd July - 6th September, 2012

Following the same premise as *Olympian Steps* but with broader international and paralympic representation, this edition was called *Golden Steps* merely in deference to tight trademark enforcement. Our route, drawing visitors between Euston and St. Pancras stations, had walls, enabling us to include events involving height as well as length.

Usain Bolt: 100m, for Jamaica, Beijing 2008.
Paola Fantato: Archery, for Italy, Sydney Paralympics 2000.
Sally Gunnell: 400m Hurdles,
for Great Britain and Northern Ireland, Barcelona 1996.
Jonathan Edwards: Triple Jump,
for Great Britain and Northern Ireland, Sydney 2000.
Arnold Boldt: High Jump, for Canada,
Arnhem Paralympics, 1980.
Ray Ewry: Standing Long jump,
for the United States of America, London 1908.
Olga Korbut: Gymnastics, for the Soviet Union, Munich 1972.

Julius Kariuki: 3000m Steeplechase, for Kenya, Seoul 1988.
Na Cui: Judo, for China, Beijing 2008.
Joaquin Capilla Perez: 10m Dive, for Mexico, Melbourne 1956.
Naim Süleymanoglu: Weightlinfting, for Turkey, Atlanta 1996.
Kamila Skolimowska: Hammer, for Poland, Sydney 2000.
A medal ceremony, London 2012.

Both the Installation and maintenance of *Golden Steps* was made challenging by regular rain but the great enthusiasm of visitors and local residents buoyed our spirits. Painting the 10m diving board on the side of a building was no fun at all.

Devised by James Yarker and Craig Stephens with Jack Trow.
Installed by Alice Greenham, Denise Stanton, Jack Trow,
Billy Wolf and James Yarker.
Administration Charlotte Martin.
Thanks to: Sarah Davies, Emma Underhill and Laura Harford.
Commissioned by Up Projects for Camden Council.
Photographs © Stan's Cafe

Foot Steps.
Wellingborough Town Centre
27th August - Early November, 2012

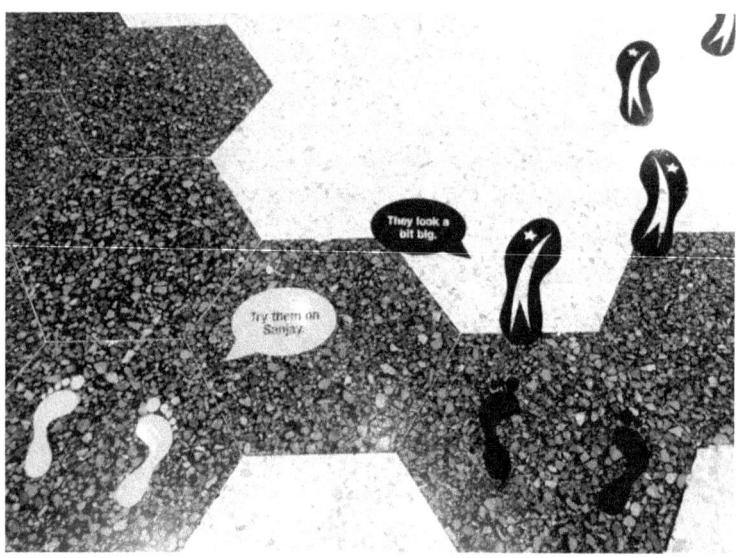

Foot Steps was commissioned for *Global Footprint*, a series of art projects celebrating Northamptonshire's shoe industry.

A tour of Wellingborough and research into its history prompted a series of scenes mixed between legacies of the shoe industry and fables from the town's past, including an April Fools Day prank in 1959, which involved someone painting white footsteps through the town centre.

For the first time we mixed indoor and outdoor elements, using vinyl and paint respectively. Encouraged by the excellent detail achieved with stencils in *Golden Steps* we increased the number of ambitious outdoor design elements in *Foot Steps*, which proved challenging when faced with the variable surfaces around the town centre. Installing on the street was time consuming but public feedback was encouraging and reminded us of people's enthusiasm for the project. When all elements were installed a Google Map was set up to help people navigate the full set.

Devised by James Yarker, Simon Ford and Denise Stanton
with Craig Stephens.
Installed by Denise Stanton, Simon Ford, Jake Oldershaw,
Alice Greenham, Chris Dugrenier, James and Eve Yarker.
Commissioned by Global Footprint,
part of the London 2012 Cultural Olympiad.
With thanks to: Swansgate Centre, The Castle Theatre,
Borough Council of Wellingborough,
Northamptonshire County Council and Graham Callister.
Photographs © Stan's Cafe.

Dragon Steps
Juice Festival - NewcastleGateshead
26th October - 4th November, 2012

Juice, is a festival for young people in NewcastleGateshead, that runs across a host of arts venues. In 2012 they commissioned an edition of *The Steps Series*. Part of the brief they gave us was to bring a greater unity to the festival by working across a number of their venues.

Seven Stories - The National Centre For Children's Books, had an exhibition celebrating Cressida Cowell's Dragon books, which prompted the whole festival to be themed around dragons, hence *Dragon Steps*.

Our narrative was a simple one. In the Great North Museum: Hancock one of its exhibits, previously thought to be a fossilised egg, hatches and out steps a baby dragon. Two children see this event. The baby dragon sets off looking for its mother, followed by the children and a suspicious museum guard. The chase goes on to cause chaos down the road at Northern Stage and further on at Dance City. In the Discovery Museum the adventure goes underwater around the big boat displayed in their main hall. Across the river at The Sage Gateshead the Dragon's mother is starting to eat people unlucky enough not to be able to make their escape and finally, from the viewing platform at the BALTIC gallery, the children and guard spot a touching dragon reunion.

Devised by Juice Volunteers - Anna, Mani, Marcus,
with Simon Ford, Denise Stanton, Craig Stephens
and James Yarker
Commissioned for Juice by Rachel Adam,
Clair Newton and Laura Cresser
Production Manager: Jill Bennison
Photographs © Stan's Cafe

Robot Steps
Weekender - The Barbican Centre, London
3rd & 4th November, 2012

The Barbican commissioned this edition for their Weekender event - Natural Circuits, which was themed on the relationship between humans and technology. *Robot Steps* tells a story of Jo, whose younger sibling Sam, looks like a child but is in fact a robot, programmed to act as both friend and guardian while Jo's parents are away.

After saying goodbye to Jo's parents the two 'children' set off to play. Jo skips around and initiates a game of tag, puts her ear to a metal pipe and imagines she can hear the sea. Sam plays along but is less imaginative. They both play hopscotch. Jo has learnt to cartwheel, but Sam never will. Sam passes messages back and forth between Jo and her mum. Jo is tripped by a pair of bullies. The bullies try to mug Jo but she has no valuables as Sam has them all and when challenged Sam gives the two attackers an electric shock. Safe again the pair set off. Sam sets up a phone line with Jo's mum before his batteries run flat.

Resourceful Jo finds a powerpoint to recharge Sam's batteries. The pair find a mirror and Sam takes their photo together. Sam guides them around a corner to reunite with Jo's parents.

On their shopping mission Jo's parents have bought their daughter a surprise, a larger, shiny new robot that can do cartwheels. Named Sam by Jo, the new friends go off together and dad takes old Sam to stand by the recycling bins. 'Click'.

Installed just for the Natural Circuits event, this was the briefest edition of *the Steps Series* but the weekend was well attended making it all worthwhile. For the shiny new Sam's feet we invested in some special reflective silver coloured vinyl.

Devised and installed by Simon Ford, Craig Stephens and
James Yarker with Denise Stanton.
Removed by: Gareth Brierly, Annie Calvery, Charlotte Martin,
Bernadette Russell and Billy Wolf.
Commissioned by: The Barbican.
Thanks to: Jenny Mollica, Emma Passmore
and Kai (for cartwheel advice).
Photos © Susan Sanroman

Exodus Steps
Skirball Cultural Centre, Los Angeles
1st March - & 28th April, 2013

"Exodus Steps is an interactive journey through the museum, and it is simultaneously so simple and so clever that it's bound to win over every member of the family. The nine-year-old I tore away from his Wii to check it out was intent on NOT enjoying himself, and yet Exodus Steps had him charmed and engaged in spite of himself in, literally, a few steps."
Mommy Poppins - Get more out of LA with kids.

The campus of Skirball Cultural Center in Los Angeles was the perfect location for what is, to date, the most ambitious and spectacular edition of the series so far. The installation was designed as an engaging way for families to explore the biblical story of Exodus, with its tone carefully pitched to be witty and playful, whilst retaining a strong sense of respect for the story's sacred origins.

Prologue: Entrance Path.
The Hebrews are enslaved in Egypt.

Scene 1: Founders Courtyard.
To avoid her baby falling into Egyptian hands a mother floats him down the river in a basket. Downstream, Pharaoh's daughter rescues the baby and names him Moses. Miriam has followed her baby brother and volunteers her mother as his nurse and thus is able to bring him home.

Scene 2: Downstairs behind reception.
Moses sees a Hebrew slave being mistreated, intervenes and in so doing kills the slave master; he must flee Egypt.

Scene 3: Outside Audry's Bookshop.
Out wandering, Moses meets seven sisters at a well, including Zapporah, his future wife.

Scene 4: The Melkin Corridor.
In the wilderness, God's voice comes from a burning bush, telling Moses he has been chosen to lead the Hebrew people to freedom.

Scene 5: Further Down The Melkin Corridor.
Returning to Egypt, Moses and his family meet Aaron, Moses' brother, who volunteers to help in the task ahead.

Scene 6: Rooftop terraces.
Moses and Aaron visit Pharaoh, explaining that their God has asked him to release the Hebrew people. Pharaoh declares that he is not afraid of the Hebrew God. A series of plagues descend on Pharaoh's people. After each plague Pharaoh grants the Hebrews freedom, only to later change his mind.

Scene 7a: In the foyer of the Getty Gallery.
Moses' family put lamb's blood on their doorposts as a sign that the tenth plague should pass over their house.

Scene 7b: Outside the lift and building.
The Hebrews run for freedom, following a pillar of cloud in the day and a pillar of fire at night.

Scene 8: The Rainbow Arbor.
Pharaoh has sent soldiers and chariots to chase the Hebrews. Trapped, Moses trusts God and parts the sea with his rod. Once the Hebrews are safely across, the waters of the sea close back in, drowning their pursuers. Aaron is astounded. Miriam celebrates by leading a dance. Moses is exhausted and a sheep contemplates its future.

Scene 9: Amphitheatre (right hand side).
In the wilderness the Hebrews are worshiping a golden model cow and Moses is up a mountain with God, being given the Ten

Commandments. Returning to camp Moses is appalled by the behaviour he finds.

Scene 10: Amphitheatre (left hand side).
The Hebrews have built a tabernacle to worship their God. The Ten Commandments are in place and thoughts turn to the future and The Promised Land.

The installation contained two treasure hunt challenges, one to find a series of symbolic objects used in the Jewish Passover ritual, the other to find a mini loaf of Hametz bread in each scene.

Devised by: Simon Ford and James Yarker.
Installed with help from Kiki Johnson and Cris Capp.
Stan's Cafe Management: Charlotte Martin.
Commissioned by: Skirball Cultural Center.
Made possible by an anonymous donor and Art Works.
Thanks to Jordan Peimer, Amina Sanchez and everyone at Skirball for their unflagging support, help and friendliness.
Photographs © BeBe Jacobs

The Orchestra Dream
Symphony Hall, Birmingham

As the title might suggest, this is a somewhat anomalous edition of *The Steps Series*. We were commissioned by Symphony Hall, Birmingham to create an installation to accompany the *Universe of Sound* installation they were running off-site across Centenary Square.

With all but the ground floor entirely covered in carpet we needed to consider a fresh approach. On the ground floor Gustav Holst is asleep, dreaming of a major new composition: The Planets. Thereafter, *The Orchestra Dream* is a vinyl treasure hunt with visitors encouraged to take a Quiz Card and scour Levels 3 - 5a of the Symphony Hall's foyers, to find all the instruments Holst needs to complete his piece. As each new instrument is found, a code letter is collected. When all 29 letters are in place they spell out a code phrase which people emailed to the Symphony Hall in order to be entered into a prize draw.

The instruments were colour coded by group e.g. Woodwind = Blue and were broadly arranged so the lowest pitched instrument of each family was sited on the lowest levels and highest pitched on the highest level.

Devised by: Craig Stephens and James Yarker
with Denise Stanton.
Design: Simon Ford.
Stan's Cafe management: Charlotte Martin.
Commissioned by: Town Hall Symphony Hall.
Thanks to: Katie Banks, Emma Nenadic, Joanna Sigsworth
and Richard Hawley.
Photographs © Stan's Cafe

St. George's Steps
Saltley Academy, Birmingham
23rd April and in school until 17th July, 2015

Saltley Academy was looking for a high profile art project that would have an impact on the whole school community and launch the school's new approach to education and engaging its students. It also wanted to find a way of responding to the Department of Education's new requirement that schools teach their students 'Modern British Values' (equality, freedom of speech, tolerance, the rule of law and community). Our response was to propose *St. George's Steps*.

St. George is interesting in this context as he wasn't born in England, never visited the country and yet is our patron Saint – as well as being the patron Saint of other countries, regions and cities. We were interested in using moments from British history to show how our values have evolved over time.

Each of eight Year 7 classes took responsibility for creating and installing a different scene, as well as developing questions for other students based on this scene.

Scene 1: Signing the Magna Carta.
Scene 2: Discovering the Gunpowder Plot.
Scene 3: Suffragettes at the Derby.
Scene 4: Ramblers demand the right to roam.
Scene 5: Sheltering in an underground station during the Blitz.
Scene 6: Playing village cricket.
Scene 7: Celebrating the Queen's Jubilee.
Scene 8: Slaying the Dragon.

A small group of students were responsible for maintaining the installation through the year and for introducing visitors to it. They were featured on the local television news.

Devised by Saltley Academy Year 7 with Simon Ford,
Denise Stanton, Jack Trow and James Yarker.
Activity sheets by Year 7 with Denise Stanton and Mr. Bentley.
Produced by Mr. Weir and Andrew Fox.
Commissioned by Saltley Academy.
Photos © Graeme Braidwood and Ming DeNasty.

Shakespeare Steps
Stratford-upon-Avon
23rd April (Shakespeare's Birthday) – 30th October, 2016

The stresses of installing *Golden Steps* led us to vow we would never do an outdoor edition in the UK again. However, when The Royal Shakespeare Company asked if we could do a modest edition based on *A Midsummer Nights Dream* in midsummer the opportunity felt contained and too good to turn down. Within a fortnight this offer had escalated to a commission from the RSC, Shakespeare's Birthplace Trust and Shakespeare's School Room for a year long version, marking the 400th Anniversary of Shakespeare's death, linking his Birthplace, along the town's 'Historic Spine' to Holy Trinity Church where he is buried and from there along the river bank to the Royal Shakespeare Theatre where his works are still performed.

Our response, based around the 'Seven Ages of Man' speech found in *As You Like It*, imagined scenes from his life and used quotes from his work, whilst referencing historical details of Stratford-Upon-Avon four hundred years ago.

Scene 1: The Infant - outside Shakespeare's Birthplace.
Scene 2: The Lover - Henley Street / Cooks Alley.
Scene 3: The Soldier - High Street / Sheep Street.
Scene 4: The Justice - Shakespeare's New Place.
Scene 5: The Schoolboy - Shakespeare's Schoolroom.
Scene 6: Old Age - Hall's Croft.
Scene 7: Death - Holy Trinity Church.
Scene 8: The Legacy - Royal Shakespeare Theatre (colonnade).

Late December 2015 and January 2016 were among the coldest and wettest weeks on record, so installation was pushed back until Spring and ran through until mid-Autumn. A map detailing the installation was made available around the town and on-line.

Devised by: Craig Stephens, Simon Ford and James Yarker.
Installed by: Graeme Rose, Denise Stanton,
Craig Stephens and Jack Trow..
Administration: Rowena Wilding. Produced by: Roisin Caffrey.
Commissioned by the Royal Shakespeare Company in
association with The Shakespeare Birthplace Trust,
Shakespeare's Schoolroom and Guildhall with support from
the Stratford Society and Guild Chapel.
Thanks to: Louisa Davies, Laura Keating, Bob Bearman,
Erin Sullivan, Amaaya, Robin, Eve, Holy Trinity Church,
Bennet Carr and Marion Morgan. Photographs © Stan's Cafe.

Banana Pyjama Ninja
Saltley Academy, Birmingham
From September 2018

The brief was to help students to learn how Britain's influence on the world is woven in with the world's influence on Britain, and to contribute to the school's focus on widening student's vocabulary.

Our aim was to give students and teachers as much creative freedom as possible in developing *Banana Pyjama Ninja*. We nudged, selected and edited their content and as a result of small group working ended up with more than twenty scenes. For the piece to be manageable some scenes had to be quite brief, but all had wit to them and included two 'star words', familiar English words, whose origin was to be researched and would be found to have origins in a different language.

Scenes were arranged in chronological order around the school's ground floor corridors. Stonehenge, Romans building roads, Viking raids, local settlements in the Domesday Book, Richard the Lion Heart not speaking English, Elizabeth 1st and

Walter Raleigh potatoes and tobacco, pilgrims flee across the Atlantic, Shakespeare writes plays, Newton and gravity, Jane Austen writes novels, Oliver Twist, Victorians 'inventing' Christmas traditions, Stephenson's Rocket, telephone communications, the origins of cricket's Ashes, Irish immigration, World War 1 and its graves, Fleming and penicillin, Windrush immigration, an early 'curry house' in England, a World Cup trophy being found by a dog in 1966, Helen Sharman in space, Malala Yousafzai's story, Prince Harry and Meghan are engaged.

Devised by: Saltley Academy Year 7, Simon Ford, Beth Kapila, Jack Trow, Laura Wynter, Amy Taylor, James Yarker.
Photographs © Stan's Cafe.

About the illustration and design

The illustrations for the covers of these books were undertaken by students at Birmingham City University as the final module of their first-year illustration course during the Spring/Summer of 2018. The images were developed using workshops using variations of the theatre-devising methods produced by Stan's Cafe but adapted and applied to the making of visual work. The resulting work was shown in the pop-up exhibition *The Something Of Somebody Something* at AE Harris in May 2018.

The design concept of the books was produced by final year Graphic Design student Aimee Chapman. These were then further developed for print in a collaborative process between Stan's Cafe and the University's Innovation Product Support Service (IPSS) and involved helping the company with selecting appropriate DTP software, undertaking training and selecting a suitable print on demand service.

Gareth Courage
Lecturer in Illustration
Birmingham City University

www.ingramcontent.com/pod-product-compliance
Lightning Source LLC
Chambersburg PA
CBHW071756080526
44588CB00013B/2255